Outlander

1983–1985

Outlander

Frederick Staver

Resource *Publications*
An imprint of *Wipf and Stock Publishers*
199 West 8th Avenue • Eugene OR 97401

Resource Publications
An imprint of Wipf and Stock Publishers
199 West 8th Avenue, Suite 3
Eugene, OR 97401

Outlander
Copyright©2005 by Sarah J. Beecroft
ISBN: 1-59752-475-1
Publication Date: December 2005

*The family of Mr. Frederick L. Staver
lovingly publish this book in his memory.*

Old men ought to be explorers
Here and there does not matter –
                    East Coker

Table of Contents

Foreword	ix
I. Toward the Trillium	1
II. Sleeping and Waking	13
III. The Outlands	23

Foreword

What I write that purports to be
poetry, if it is to make adequate
sense, may do so when heard. Those
who chance to read and don't wish
to voice it, to them I say, skip
the poems and turn to something else.

I.
Toward the Trillium

Toward the Trillium

1

Autumn toward winter.
The lonely bird of self
hungers, pillages
last seeds in the shrunken
yellow rind.

Time now of the sour rains,
dying mirrors,
the guitar's song,
promise of radiant suns.

Frederick Staver

2

A morning of slant snow.
The harbor, its slips
where the flakes dissolve –
oil slicks, feathers, orange peels,
rust.
Forgotten now the names
of ships that berthed there;
cranes with noosed slings,
skeletal fingers against
a frozen sky,
and the way back whiteness,
a muffled drumbeat.

On a piling, aloof,
a phantom gull.

Toward the Trillium

3

Murmuring what to yourself
these winter hours?
The headlights of the cars
infiltrate shadows
along the asphalt strip.
And the broken lines of light
fade into districts where
avenues stream with emptiness,
places where the night is final
and children sleep.

What can you say?
The god of energy spears
from the moving lamps,
circles the crossings, leaps
through the wilderness of strung wires,
bathes in the city flare.
And the river coiling
under frosty light
glitters beyond the bridges, slides
north into dark.
                        The god

leaps in you.

Frederick Staver

4

The human shadow
sprawling across all landscapes
creates a partial eclipse.
In so much artificial light
you can't make out this darkness.
Yet it is there.

But the hawk,
tethered to his fields,
burns with the sun,
free.

Toward the Trillium

5

There is no argument.
Always the open way
to the city, the mountains,
the sea.
You are not what you were,
and the solitude echoes.

Frederick Staver

6

In the city, snow
on the cornices, the statues.
Lamp posts wear white caps.
Strangers I'll never know
pass me like shadows,
zippered against the cold.
Going they go
as we must go,
our alien bodies
bent to the weather.
We glance at times at the sky.
And the wintry sun
nourishes darkness.
Locked into urban geometry,
eyes bleed cold.

Toward the Trillium

7

Day losing the valley runs
on legs of the long shadows.
I plod a scarred slope
up to thinness –
hairline of snow.
At oceanside the wind
whistles me down:
What are you doing here
in the off-season?
Admiring old age,
the wrinkles of the sea.

Rejoice!

Frederick Staver

8

Let joy be
the final imperative,
through the fir needle,
trillium, the star
dog your heart
with the singleness of things.
Gathering yourself
as for a journey,
lift up to the circling
hawk, catch joy
from the waternets flung
over pockmarked stone –
nets crafted instantly
that snare the gull's shadow.

At other times
consult your pulse and the sun.
Only then enter the marts
where everything is for sale:
synthetic skirts, gunmetal flowers.

Toward the Trillium

9

The world you knew,
the one you believed in,
recedes, vanishes into history.

And no return.

To the hawk, the seagull, the self,
although the forms change
and the god of energy leaps high,
yester and future are the same.

II.
Sleeping and Waking

Sleeping and Waking

1

An arrowhead of geese
strikes toward the north –
a victorious sign.
And a spring-in-winter sun
promises,
snowdrops at my feet.

Frederick Staver

2

Following the water,
its crooked way
down forested miles,
out of the lostness of hills
I come to the farms –
sunlight and labor.
Tractors crawl the fields,
discs trailing duststorms;
their drivers steer
toward a green world.

Now a night without sleep.
I lean to the window, stare
out at the dark warrens
of a technical culture.
What is a good life?
Does anyone know?
And I think of the outlands
under massive night,
where sleeping farms wait
for star-wane, empty dawn,
cockcrow.

Sleeping and Waking

3

Along the park's edge
motors troll by,
humming unerringly
of us, of our time.

They are our music.

A butterfly staggers
over azaleas,
inebriate in its flight.

How can it tell
it is out of tune?

And a tumult of sparrows,
tempo rubato,
pipes austral hours,
snug in green.

I relax, listen,
when out of the sun
a thundering staccato!
Trees go silent
at a whirlibird's chop.

Frederick Staver

4

Everything speaks,
even inanimate things,
though not with the same tongue.
You can hear them
if you choose to listen:
the language of speech,
that of silence.

Who listens now?

Crow high on a crossarm
balances,
utters his word.
He sees me, sheds me,
flaps heavily away.

Sleeping and Waking

And I stroll into the wind,
below the city towers
that manage the sun.
I look up, listen
to intuit their silence:
"Admire us, we stand tall,
in the corporate life
impeccable.
From our overlook
we monitor the times,
finger their pulse,
make the decisions.
And you – what are you?
Only a man."

Frederick Staver

5

Alone in this house of strangers,
with its limitless horizons,
and yet – not alone.
Speak to the one in the mirror:
I becomes you.

And you smile – you
a dust grain in the wind,
humanly charged with
the incorrigible I.

Sleeping and Waking

6

On the plaza
Sunday strollers entertain
the otherness of each other
in social masks.
Couples passim
saunter the citron noon;
and while they chant
the ritual of bonhomie,
legs carelessly
scatter the pigeons.

Friday, at the rush hour,
on a deserted lot,
general selfhood
bore witness to a murder.
Anonymous blood spilled
under a knife,
and no one moved,
no one spoke a word.
Today it is pigeons,
the bobbing pigeons.

Witnesses everywhere,
bland Argus eyes
intent on tomorrow.
They see, they do not know.

Frederick Staver

7

The dark is against you,
yet you bring no light.
Privacy is a closed door.
You lie half awake
in your cube of silence,
neon frosting the pane,
crickets in the wind.

There in the dark,
the alone of your life,
a planet turns
through weather of all fortunes,
and you recognize it:
image of a world
where men build walls
and God is a shadow.
You are here and far away.

The image fails
in distances of sleep,
as men diminish
in the shadows of their machines.

Sleeping and Waking

8

You go, come, you return,
<u>here and there does not matter</u>.
Reach any terminus,
antipodal places,
the center is you.
And for you now
there is no release,
only the condition
of being as you are.

III.
The Outlands

The Outlands

1

To make a world
we unmake another,
and there are two.
Who understands this?
Who will consider it?

Possibly no one.

Frederick Staver

2

Under the sun-swarm
I stretch prone on a hill
and crane high.
Alone in the rays
a black cross floats,
merciless life at watch,
confident in its wings.
Musing, I peer
through the lens of a hawk's eye
at the earth below,
where random particles move
at work, at play,
on the holistic lap.

In this bright hour
August's seminal light humors
the ease of sunning bodies, flesh
of mine and yet not mine.

The Outlands

3

Words, many words, and more,
the common way of approximation,
and yet they shape us,
we bear their stamp
now and after we're gone.
I take to the road
(Why not in such weather?),
leave the white city,
its smiles and its bones,
the invisible walls.

Frederick Staver

4

<u>Take any road to find the quest,</u>
<u>Embrace the dayshine, name it dear.</u>
Well, no one in his right mind
would dip wings to such counsel.
But needing the deception of horizons,
you chose one – a road,
and you followed it to its end
and the sixth age, shrunken.
Strange now to think,
those lines were written
forty-odd years ago.

The Outlands

5

As the list of the dead grows
the circle narrows,
and it is age.
You count them on both hands
as you enter the forest's
primitive silences,
its reminiscence of day.

Frederick Staver

6

In memory somewhere
a guitar sings
the purposelessness of being.
It is an old song.
A thrush flutters,
dips a light bough
where the sun strikes
through needles and leaves.
You rehearse another season:
violets and storms appeared,
spring's labor then
forcing sap and blood
in the program for living.

A house for owls and deer,
this ramshackle wood
leaves you no place
with the vines, moss, shadows
of a reckless summer,
and you think about it.
No place. You are alone.

The Outlands

And you try to understand
placelessness,
the cycle and the need,
thankful for your life
in the other wilderness
half understood
and avid for power.

Frederick Staver

7

A chainsaw roars
its challenge to the forest,
waking a mountain.

A log truck labors
a dusty hillside road,
hauling dismembered trees.

Somewhere in thin cloud
an airliner's twin jets
shorten its horizons.

Silence is your silence.
On the outlands of spirit
machines cannot follow.

The Outlands

8

Near the dark edge now,
you cross September fields,
slow as a shadeline,
lean as water,
and the trouble is age.

Frederick Staver

9

Summer forgets this land,
its diminuendo
ends in emptiness
under blue miles – vacancy
rinsed by wind.
Time now to let go everything
unworthy of remembrance;
a time to forsake
both the labor and joy
on the high wire
of imagination.

Having known love,
accept yourself as you are.
For the rest:
the appetite of audiences,
vague posturing before mirrors,
a study of appearances –
the world.

www.ingramcontent.com/pod-product-compliance
Lightning Source LLC
Chambersburg PA
CBHW061516040426
42450CB00008B/1646